Dreams and Their Interpretation

By Astra Cielo

Copyright © 2020 Lamp of Trismegistus. All rights reserved. No part of this publication may be reproduced or transmitted in any form or by any means, electronic or mechanical, including photocopying, recording, or by any information storage and retrieval system, without permission in writing from Lamp of Trismegistus. Reviewers may quote brief passages.

ISBN: 978-1-63118-468-0

Esoteric Classics

Other Books in this Series and Related Titles

Fortune-Telling with Dice by Astra Cielo (978-1-63118-466-6)

Fortune-Telling by Playing Cards by Astra Cielo (978-1-63118-467-3)

History, Analysis and Secret Tradition of the Tarot by Manly P. Hall, A. E. Waite &c (978-1-63118-445-1)

Crystal Vision Through Crystal Gazing by Achad (978-1-63118-455-0)

Magical Essays and Instructions by Florence Farr (978-1-63118-418-5)

Ancient Mysteries and Secret Societies by Hall (978-1-63118-410-9)

The Path of Light: A Manual of Maha-Yana Buddhism by L. D. Barnett (978-1-63118-471-0)

The Rosicrucian Chemical Marriage by Christian Rosenkreuz (978-1-63118-458-1)

Ghosts in Solid Form by Gambier Bolton (978-1-63118-469-7)

American Indian Freemasonry by A. C. Parker (978-1-63118-460-4)

The Mysteries of Freemasonry & the Druids by Albert G. Mackey, Manly P. Hall &c (978-1-63118-444-4)

The Legend of the Holy Grail and its Connection with Templars and Freemasons by A. E. Waite (978-1-63118-462-8)

Arcane Formulas or Mental Alchemy by William Walker Atkinson (978-1-63118-459-8)

The Machinery of the Mind by Dion Fortune (978-1-63118-451-2)

The Gospel of the Nativity of Mary by St. Matthew (978-1-63118-448-2)

Buddhist Psalms by Shinran (978-1-63118-465-9)

Audio Versions are also Available on Audible and iTunes

Table of Contents

Introduction…7

Dreams and Their Interpretation…9

Do Dreams Foretell the Future?…12

How Dreams Should be Interpreted…15

A Dictionary of Dreams…17

INTRODUCTION

The word "esoteric" can be difficult to define. Esotericism in general can be seen less as a system of beliefs and more as a category, which encompasses numerous, different systems of beliefs. It's a bit of juxtaposition, since the word "esoteric" indicates something that few people know about, while the term itself broadly covers numerous philosophies, practices, areas of study and belief systems.

In a greater sense, Esotericism acts as a storehouse for secret knowledge, which is often considered ancient (by *tradition, if not by fact),* passed down from generation to generation, in private. At various times in history, simply possessing the knowledge of some of these subjects, was considered illegal and a jailable offence, if discovered. This usually included such general topics as Alchemy, Qabalah, Hermeticism, Occultism, Ceremonial Magic, Astrology, Divination, Rosicrucianism and so on. Collectively, these areas of study were often referred to as the esoteric sciences.

Sometimes, the outer garment of a subject isn't esoteric, while what is hidden beneath it, is. As an example, Freemasonry isn't necessarily esoteric by nature (at *least not anymore),* but certain signs, passwords and handshakes given to the candidate during their initiation, are in fact, esoteric, in the sense that they are hidden from the general public.

Today, in the twenty-first century, such topics are readily available at bookstores across the country, and numerous mainsteam publishers offer beginners guides and coffee-table volumes on many of these subjects, intended for mass appeal. Books like *"The Secret"* have turned previously arcane topics into household knowledge. All that being the case, however, it isn't to say that there still aren't buried secrets to uncover, ancient wisdom being ignored and forgotten mysteries to be explored. In fact, it is often that we are only able to further our own studies by standing on the shoulders of these disappearing giants.

Lamp of Trismegistus is doing its part to help preserve humanity's esoteric history by making some of these classics available to those students who are seeking to unearth the knowledge of these ancient colossi.

So, be sure to check other titles from our *Esoteric Classics* series, as well as our *Occult Fiction, Theosophical Classics, Foundations of Freemasonry Series, Supernatural Fiction, Paranormal Research Series, Studies in Buddhism* and our *Christian Apocrypha Series*. You can also download the audio versions of most of these titles from iTunes or Audible, for learning on the go.

DREAMS AND THEIR INTERPRETATION

Dreams are the thoughts or impressions that occupy our minds when we are asleep.

Every night, unless disease or strong excitement prevent, we are the subject of a phenomenon which if it only occurred once in a lifetime we would consider one of the greatest mysteries. We pass in an unconscious moment from the usual world of deed and action into another world, where we are unaware of what goes on around us; where we see, not with the eyes, where we hear things of which the ear gives no impression; in which we speak and are spoken to, although no speech passes our lips or reaches our organs of hearing.

In that world we are excited to joy, to grief; we are moved to pity, we are stirred to anger; and yet these emotions are aroused by things that do not exist. Time seems to have lost its landmarks; distance offers no barriers; the dead return and the past comes once again to cheer or to grieve us.

We live in a land of Dreams. Many of the thoughts that pass thru our brains are forgotten before we awake. It often happens that people talk in their sleep, thus proving that they are dreaming, but on being awakened they deny that they dreamed, for their dreams have left no trace upon their memory.

The question whether we ever sleep without dreaming is as old as the days of the ancient Greek philosophers, and there are many able authorities on both sides of the question.

Locke, a great writer on mental phenomena, is of the opinion that dreaming is not always present during sleep; but many of the ancient as well as the modern writers contend that the mind is never at rest but continues uninterruptedly even in sleep, and that to cease to dream would be to cease to live.

Sir William Hamilton argues as follows: "When we dream, we are assuredly asleep, but the mind is not asleep, because it thinks. It is therefore manifest that mental processes may go on even though the body is unconscious. To have no recollection of our dreams does not prove that we have not dreamed, although the dream may have left no trace on our memories."

Dreams, like our waking thoughts, are dependent on the laws of association. Although the senses, are usually torpid in sleep, some of them continue to transmit to the mind imperfect sensations which they receive. Experiments have been tried to determine how far external impressions will cause dreams. A bottle of hot water applied to the feet of a sleeping man caused him to dream that he was on the crater of a volcano and that the hot earth was scorching his feet. Another man, having a blister applied to his head, dreamed that he was being scalped by Indians. A match suddenly lit may cause a man to dream of a terrible storm with lightning and thunder. Darwin relates the case of a man who was born deaf and dumb, and who never dreamed that he conversed with others except thru the sign language. So, also, a blind man never dreams of seeing vivid colors. Thus we see that our dreams are in many cases dependent upon our senses.

The condition of our digestion may also influence our dreams. If the digestive functions are properly performed, our dreams are apt to be pleasant, whereas everyone knows the torturing dreams that may follow an indigestible supper of Welsh rabbit or lobster. In the same way the dreams that are caused by opium or other drugs or by intoxicating liquors are apt to be of a disagreeable nature.

The mind works with wonderful rapidity during sleep. A person who is suddenly awakened by a loud noise may dream of many things in the short second before he awakens. A long story may spin itself out in his brain,—adventure, robbery, war,—until he is awakened by what he believes is a shot. A certain writer was suddenly aroused from a sound sleep by a few drops of water sprinkled on his face. He dreamed of the events of an entire life in which sorrow and happiness were mingled, of a fight on the banks of a stream into which an enemy plunged him. We can dream more in a minute of time than we can enact in a day.

So, too, dreams are often characteristic of the peculiar life and thoughts of the dreamer. A miser will dream of saving money, a merchant of business deals, a musician of melody, etc. As a general thing our dreams are wanting in coherence. They do not seem true to life. They mix together things that are absurd and unconnected. We never dream of the past as a thing that is past, but as a reality. People that are long dead appear to us as living.

Do Dreams Foretell the Future?

It is a popular belief, and has been thru all ages, that dreams foretell for us what will happen. Many remarkable cases seem to prove this. All nations of antiquity believed in the divine nature of dreams. The Bible is full of allusions to dreams and most of the important events were revealed to men thru dreams.

Jacob dreamed that he saw a ladder which reached into the sky and that angels were ascending and descending. His whole life was shaped by this vision. His son, Joseph, was called "The Dreamer" by his brothers. We all know the fascinating story of his dreams, his interpretations of the visions of the butler and the baker and his reading of Pharaoh's dream which eventually obtained for him the position of ruler over Egypt. The Books of the Prophets and of Daniel are based on dreams. So are many of the incidents of the New Testament.

Coming down to more modern times, we find that many intelligent men—writers, inventors, kings—believed in dreams.

Franklin believed that he obtained a clearer insight into political events thru his dreams and often acted upon the inspiration he received while asleep.

A celebrated doctor discovered a well-known remedy thru a dream. Tartini, a celebrated musician, is said to have composed his "Devil's Sonata" under the inspiration of a dream in which the devil appeared to him and invited him to try his skill upon his favorite fiddle. When he awoke, the music was so firmly impressed upon his memory that he had no difficulty in writing it out on paper.

The poet Coleridge is said to have composed his poem "Kubla Khan" in a dream. He had taken an anodyne for some slight indisposition, and fell asleep in his chair. When he awoke he retained the impression of over two hundred lines of verse which had come to him in his slumber.

Cabanis, the philosopher, found in his sleep the conclusions of many problems that he was not able to solve while awake. Condorcet, the mathematician, found in his sleep the final steps in a calculation that baffled him while awake.

Napoleon was a great believer in dreams and was often guided by them in his campaigns.

Columbus, it is said, dreamed that a voice spoke to him saying, "God will give thee the keys of the gates of the Ocean," and that it was this that kept up his courage.

In remote times the greatest of importance was attached to dreams. The ancients resorted to them in cases of difficulty or calamity. When pestilence spread among the Greeks before Troy, Homer represents Achilles as taking refuge in dreams, his reason being,—

"Dreams descend from Jove."

Aristotle, Plato, Zeno, Pythagoras, Socrates, Xenophon and Sophocles have all expressed their belief in the divine or prophetic character of dreams.

A great number of historical instances are recorded in Greek and Latin classics of dreams that came true. The night before the assassination of Julius Cæsar, his wife Calpurnia dreamed that her husband fell bleeding across her knees. She tried to warn him, but he laughed at her fears. On the night that Attila died, the Emperor Marcian at Constantinople dreamed that he saw the bow of the conqueror broken asunder. Cicero relates a dream thru which a murderer was brought to justice.

Dreams were even allowed to influence legislation. During the Marsic War (90 B.C.) the Roman senate ordered the temple of Juno to be rebuilt, in consequence of a dream. There are many other examples in ancient history.

The old fathers of the Christian Church attached considerable importance to dreams. Tertullian thought they came from God as one of a series of prophecy, though he attributed many dreams to the influence of evil spirits. St. Augustine relates a dream thru which he was convinced of the immortality of the soul.

How Dreams Should be Interpreted

There are two kinds of dreams: those that are reproductions of one's waking thoughts or actions, or the result of digestive disturbances; and those that proceed from some psychological condition which we cannot probe or understand. Many dreams are of so trivial a nature that it would be foolish to attribute any importance to them. Others seems to come from some outside inspiration and are prophetic. The ancient sages who were celebrated as interpreters of dreams had a maxim that the "Result of dreams often follows their interpretation." They meant that if you believe that a dream means a certain thing, you will fashion your actions so that that thing will come true.

When the meaning of a dream is indefinite, many interpretations can be put on it and all of them be capable of coming true. If you are told that a dream means illness, you may take it so to heart that you will actually fall ill, or if you are philosophical, you will shape your diet or your deeds so that good health may result from the warning. If a man dreams that he will have financial disaster, he may become so unfitted thru fear that he will neglect his business and thus invite the ruin which he imagines the dream foretold. Or he may, if he is wise, take the opposite course and so shape his business methods that success will follow instead of ruin.

In the following tables we give the interpretations of common dreams as they are and have been given from time immemorial in most of the best-known sources, with quite a number of original meanings as experience has shown them to us. Remember that the interpretation of dreams may vary with the peculiar conditions and circumstances surrounding the dreamer, and what would be true in the case of a sickly person might have the opposite meaning in the case of a robust man. "Man is master of his fate," says a poet. The troubles that cause one person to take a pessimistic attitude and contemplate suicide serve to spur another on to new endeavors and new successes.

This book is not intended to foster superstition, but to offer a means of solving many of the mysterious occurrences in our lives and help you rise above your surroundings to a higher plane of usefulness.

A DICTIONARY OF DREAMS

As a rule dreams are very complex and it is difficult to single out any particular feature that stands forth and dominates the dream. But it frequently happens that one idea is so vivid that it is remembered to the exclusion of all the rest. When you have a dream of this kind refer at once to the following list, look up the dominant thought of your dream and the interpretation will be given. These meanings are not random guesses, but are compiled from a number of very old books which have come down to us from such seers, astrologers and psychologists as Cagliostro, Lenormand, Albertus Magnus and others. Of course the meaning of the dream may be considerably modified by what subconscious thoughts accompany the dream. Thus while pearls may represent tears, yet if they are accompanied by the idea of love the indication is favorable, and means a gift of affection.

A

Abandoned—Dreaming that you are deserted by your friends denotes their affection and love, but to dream that you have abandoned someone you love is a sign of disappointment.

Abbey—The ruins of an abbey mean good fortune; if seen by moonlight, wealth.

Abroad—Dreaming that you are in a strange land signifies success in your undertakings.

Absence—To be absent from home means a joyful reunion. To see people who are absent foretells speedy return.

Abundance—To dream of abundance shows a false security.

Account—A bank account signifies bankruptcy.

Acorns—Are a sign of loss of money or of love.

Almonds—If you dream of eating them it denotes an evil from which you will escape.

Alms—Giving alms denotes good fortune, receiving alms means loss of money.

Altar—Denotes a speedy marriage to the one you love. If already married, renewed prosperity.

Anchor—Denotes a successful enterprise.

Angel—To see an angel means a long voyage and success.

Angry—If you are angry, it portends an enemy.

Antelope—A speedy recovery from illness.

Ants—A colony of ants signifies industry leading to wealth. One ant means a disappointment.

Anvil—Seeing or hearing an anvil means happiness.

Ape—Means an enemy. If running from you, safety.

Apples—Signify gain. If you are eating them, disappointment; if on a tree, good news.

Apricots—If you dream of eating them, it means good news; if you see them on the tree or otherwise, a pleasant surprise.

Arbor—To be in an arbor means disappointment in love.

Argument—To hold an argument with anyone means that justice will be done.

Arm—To dream of breaking or injuring an arm signifies sudden fortune to a friend.

Army—To be marching with an army means "Beware of a false friend." If encamped, it means speedy success.

Artichokes—Signify embarrassment or pain.

Artist—Means that your love suit will be successful.

Ashes—Signify embarrassment and loss.

Asparagus—To eat it, means success and health.

Ass—Signifies a quarrel or scandal.

Aunt—Portends wealth from an unexpected source.

Authority—Signifies better times.

B

Baby—To hold one means true love; to rock one, embarrassment.

Bagpipe—To hear or play a bagpipe signifies trouble.

Baker—To see or speak to a baker means plenty.

Baking—If you dream of baking pies or cakes, a visitor; if bread, a loss.

Ball—Dancing at a ball means harmony and pleasure. Playing ball signifies loss of money.

Balloon—To go up in a balloon means unexpected fortune. To see one means a message from home.

Bank—Depositing in a bank, beware of loss; drawing money out a bank, trouble at home.

Barber—Being shaved by a barber, a long journey.

Barley—To dream of barley in the field means health and fortune.

Barn—If full, a happy marriage; if empty, poverty.

Barracks—To see soldiers in a barracks means peace and prosperity.

Basin—An empty basin foretells a loss; a full basin, unexpected wealth.

Basket—A full basket means ease and prosperity. An empty one means new endeavor in order to achieve success.

Bathing—Signifies happiness; in a pond, it means misfortune; in a running brook, it means disappointment.

Bat—If flying, means a quarrel with a friend; if at rest, pleasure.

Battlefield—Signifies great honor.

Beans—If cooked, they signify a quarrel; if raw, danger.

Bear—Seeing a bear foretells misfortune.

Bed—To see a strange bed means trouble; to sleep in a bed, good luck.

Beer—Signifies unfruitful endeavor.

Bees—To catch or watch them means success; to be stung by them, failure.

Beggar—To give alms means an unforeseen present; to be a beggar, unexpected health.

Bell—Hearing the marriage bell means happiness; a church bell, alarm or misfortune. A dinner bell means a feast or wedding.

Bench—To sit on a bench, "Beware of a rival."

Bereavement—Losing a relative or friend signifies a visit.

Betrothal—Foretells pleasures that may be brief.

Bible—To see a Bible is a reproach for evil deeds. To read a Bible, luck.

Billiards—Means loss thru dissipation.

Birds—Seeing birds of any kind foretells trouble and annoyance. If singing, however, they bring tidings of new pleasure.

Biscuit—Eating a biscuit denotes rejoicing.

Bite—To bite anyone signifies trouble. To be bitten signifies treachery of a supposed friend.

Blackbird—Foretells scandal and deceit.

Blindness—To lead a blind person means success in love. To dream of being blind means you will receive valuable information.

Blood—To see blood signifies a faithful lover.

Blows—To give or receive blows means forgiveness for wrongs done.

Boat—To row in a canoe or boat signifies an inheritance of money.

Boil—To suffer from a boil means unforeseen difficulty.

Bonnet—To wear a new bonnet means rivalry.

Book—Reading a book signifies failure; to give a book means victory over an enemy.

Boots—To dream of new boots means success in business; of old boots, a quarrel.

Bottles—A full bottle signifies sickness; an empty one, melancholy.

Brandy—Signifies "Beware of trouble!"

Bread—To dream of eating bread denotes profit in business.

Briars—Signify disputes.

Bricks—Signify a happy marriage and prosperity.

Bridge—To pass one means success. To fall from one, loss of business. To walk over a bridge, good fortune. To walk under one, disappointment.

Brook—Domestic happiness and friendship.

Bugs—Signify an enemy who wishes to harm you.

Bull—Denotes unexpected gain.

Butcher—Foretells sorrow thru the loss of a friend.

C

Cabbage—Indicates long life and happiness.

Cage—To dream of a cage with bird means liberty; empty it means servitude.

Cakes—Denote prosperity.

Calf—Is a sign of assured success.

Camel—Seeing one means riches; riding on one, disappointment.

Candle—A lighted candle signifies unexpected favor. An unlighted one means "Beware of trouble!"

Candy—To make or eat candy signifies good luck.

Cane—Signifies dissipation and waste.

Captive—To dream that you are in prison is a sign of luck.

Cards—To play cards means a successful marriage.

Carpenter—Denotes a new turn among business affairs.

Cart—Indicates sickness; with a horse before it, disgrace.

Carving—To dream of carving meat means business prosperity.

Cat—A white cat means a gift; a black cat means deceit or quarrel.

Cave—To be in a cave denotes loss.

Cellar—To be in a dark cellar means sickness or absence from home.

Cemetery—To be in a cemetery foretells the death of a friend.

Chain—Foretells a union of people hitherto separated.

Cheese—Foretells success and a journey.

Cherries—To eat cherries denotes love. To gather them, faithfulness.

Chess—To play a game of chess foretells business troubles.

Chestnuts—Denote troubles at home.

Chicken—To cook a chicken means good news; to eat one, arrival of a friend.

Child—To dream of children in health denotes pleasure and fortune; if ill, the dream is a warning.

Church—Signifies good fortune and many friends.

Cider—To drink cider denotes a dispute.

City—To be in a strange city means a speedy marriage.

Clams—Denote closeness and parsimony.

Clock—Seeing or hearing a clock denotes marriage.

Coal—Seeing or burning coal signifies persecution.

Cobbler—To dream of one mending shoes means trouble in money matters.

Cock—A crowing cock denotes sudden trouble.

Coffee—Drinking coffee is a sign of heavy trouble.

Coffin—Denotes a speedy marriage.

Cooking—To dream that you are cooking indicates a wedding.

Corkscrew—Means vexation; if in a bottle, trouble.

Corn—Is significant of riches and abundance.

Corpse—To dream of a dead body denotes long life, also news from friends.

Cow—Is significant of prosperity and abundance.

Crab—To see a crab walking means that your endeavors will come to naught.

Cradle—Indicates an increase in the family.

Cricket—Is a sign of hospitality and a visit.

Crocodile—Indicates a catastrophe.

Cross—To see a cross is a sign of tranquility.

Crow—Means humiliation and disgrace.

Crowd—You will receive good news.

Crutches—Indicate losses if you gamble.

Cucumber—Is a sign of serious illness.

Cypress—Foretells the death of a loved one.

D

Dancing—Indicates a handsome present of someone you love.

Debts—To dream of owing money means business safety.

Devil—To dream of the devil is a warning to turn over a new leaf.

Dice—To dream of dice indicates scandal and dishonor.

Dirt—Denotes sickness.

Dishes—Breaking dishes denotes a family quarrel.

Dispute—Among friends, indicates renewed friendship.

Ditch—To dream of seeing or falling into a ditch foretells bankruptcy.

Dog—To see a dog indicates faithfulness of a friend. To be bitten means treachery.

Door—An open door means opportunity; a closed door, adventure.

Dove—Means happiness at home.

Drawing—Indicates a rejection of marriage.

Drowning—To dream of drowning means good news from abroad; to rescue a drowning person is a sign of happiness.

Drum—To see or hear a drum indicates a trifling loss.

Drunk—To see a drunken person means bad news; to be drunk means disgrace.

Duck—Is a sign of profit and pleasure.

Duel—To fight a duel means dissension.

Dwarf—Signifies "Beware of foes!"

E

Eagle—Is a sign of worthy ambition.

Eating—To dream of eating means a happy marriage or a rich inheritance.

Eclipse—To see an eclipse means a loss in business.

Eels—Are sign of vexation.

Eggs—Eating eggs indicates a journey.

Elephant—To ride an elephant means that you will be called upon to do a service.

Elopement—Signifies a speedy marriage after trouble.

Embroidery—Signifies love and ambition.

Engaged—To dream of being engaged is a sign of a quarrel with someone you love.

Euchre—To play euchre signifies failure in business.

Eyes—To dream of eyes is a portent of bad luck.

F

Face—To dream of a smiling face indicates joy.

Failure—To dream of failure in business or in love means that you will soon be successful.

Falling—To dream of falling means a sudden improvement in your condition.

Fan—Is a sign of rivalry between women.

Farewell—To dream of parting is a sure sign of a lawsuit.

Farmer—To dream of a farmer denotes an increase in earnings.

Feast—To be seated at a feast means that there is trouble ahead.

Feathers—White feathers mean friendship; dark feathers, loss.

Field—To walk in a field means visitors.

Figs—To eat figs is a sign of interrupted pleasures.

Fingers—To dream of injured fingers denotes grief.

Fire—To see a house on fire is a sign of caution. Beware of false friends. To kindle a fire denotes anger.

Fish—To catch fish means success in business; to eat fish means beware of deceitful friends.

Flag—To see a flag means coming trouble in business; to carry one, means unexpected honor.

Flame—To see a flame is a sign of good news.

Flea—Is a sign of triumph over one's enemies.

Flood—To dream of a flood is a sign of misfortune.

Flowers—To dream of flowers is a sure sign of success in business or love.

Flute—To play or hear a flute means news of a birth.

Fly—To dream of flies is a warning that someone is jealous of us.

Fog—To be lost in a fog is a warning of coming trouble.

Fountain—To see a running fountain denotes health and abundance.

Fox—Signifies triumph over enemies.

Frog—Is a sign of vexation and annoyance.

Funeral—To see or attend a funeral is a sign of a birth or marriage.

Fur—To wear fur signifies long life and happiness.

G

Gallows—To see a gallows is a sign of dignity, honor and wealth.

Gambling—Is a warning against deception.

Garden—To walk in a garden denotes a bright future.

Garlic—Signifies deception by a woman.

Garter—To find a garter foretells a letter or a happy marriage.

Ghost—To dream of seeing a ghost means beware of sickness.

Gift—To receive a present denotes danger.

Gloves—To buy or wear gloves means a new-found friend.

Goat—To dream of a white goat means prosperity; of a black goat, sickness.

Gold—Dreaming of gold denotes profit and success. A bag of gold indicates a gain.

Grain—A field of ripe grain is a sign of prosperity.

Grapes—To see or eat grapes denotes enjoyment and plenty.

Grass—Indicates long life.

Grasshopper—Means loss of savings.

Grave—To look into an open grave means the loss of a friend. To sit near a grave is a sign of good luck.

Guitar—Means deception and treachery.

H

Hail—To dream that you are in a hailstorm denotes trouble and sadness.

Hair—To comb your hair is a sign of perplexity and anxiety.

Ham—To eat ham is a sign of happiness.

Hammock—To lie in a hammock indicates a speedy marriage.

Harp—To dream of a harp means the death of a dear one.

Harvest—Denotes wealth and abundance.

Heart—To dream of heart trouble indicates danger. The picture of a heart means true love.

Heaven—To dream that you or someone else is in heaven is a sign of peace and prosperity.

Hell—To dream of the infernal regions is a warning to reform.

Hen—A sign of profit.

Hermit—Denotes a treacherous friend.

Hill—Going up a hill means success; going down one, failure.

Hog—To dream of a hog is a lucky dream for speculators, but unlucky for lovers.

Hole—Falling into a hole is a sign of many obstacles.

Honey—Signifies success in business.

Horse—Seeing a white horse means unexpected fortune. A black horse means deceit. Riding a horse means reciprocated love.

Hotel—To stop at a hotel means success.

House—To be in a new or strange house is a sign of consolation.

Hunger—Is a sign of profitable employment.

Husband—For a wife to dream of her husband betokens a quarrel. If the dream is pleasant it may mean an agreeable surprise.

I

Ice—Denotes gratitude.

Imp—Is an occasion on which to exercise caution.

Infant—Happiness in the married state.

Ink—To upset an ink bottle is a sign of someone attempting to injure you.

Insanity—To dream of being insane is a sign that you are overworked.

Iron—To dream of a flatiron denotes that you will go thru a cruel experience.

Island—To be on an island in the ocean means luck; in a lake or river, loneliness.

Ivory—Is a sign of profitable enterprise.

Ivy—Denotes a happy termination of courtship and a fortunate marriage.

J

Jail—To be in jail or prison is a sign that you will have unexpected honor bestowed.

Jewels—To wear much jewelry indicates coming poverty; to see it on another foretells a lawsuit.

Joy—To experience great joy is a sign that you will have bad news.

Judge—Is a sign of coming punishment.

Jug—Indicates the acquaintance of a great man.

K

Key—A bunch of keys denotes treachery on the part of a supposed friend. A single key means loss.

Kill—To kill a person denotes a coming quarrel.

King—To see a king denotes satisfaction in business.

Kiss—To receive a kiss denotes that you will be betrayed. To kiss another means good news from a friend.

Kitchen—To be in a kitchen denotes the coming of visitors.

Kite—To see or fly a kite denotes failure in your plans.

Knife—Denotes inconstancy and dissension in your family.

Knitting—Is a sign of mischievous talk on the part of friends.

Knocks—Denote embarrassment and difficulties.

L

Ladder—To go up a ladder means success; to go down, humiliation.

Lake—A warning to be careful.

Lamb—This is a favorable sign to single people and indicates courtship.

Lame Person—To dream of seeing a cripple or lame person means business misfortune.

Lamp—To carry a lamp means trouble; to upset one, loss.

Lantern—To carry a lantern means a safe adventure.

Laughter—To laugh heartily in your sleep, "Beware of trouble!"

Lawyer—Dreaming of a lawyer denotes the marriage of a dear friend.

Leaves—Dry leaves are a sign of indisposition which will not last long.

Letter—To receive a letter usually means good news and prosperity.

Lettuce—Denotes poverty.

Lightning—Indicates a quarrel among lovers.

Lily—A sign of innocence and happiness.

Lion—To dream of a lion means unexpected honor.

Lizard—Seeing a lizard indicates coming trouble.

Lottery—To dream of winning money in a lottery means loss.

Lovers—To see two lovers spoon is an indication of domestic trouble.

M

Macaroni—Eating macaroni is a sign of abundance.

Manure—Indicates depravity.

Map—To see or consult a map indicates a journey.

Market—Going to market is a sign of a joyous event.

Mask—To wear a mask or see someone else wear one indicates hypocrisy.

Meat—To eat or cook meat is a sign of a big reception.

Melon—Signifies hope and success.

Milestone—Seeing a milestone indicates a successful venture.

Milk—Dreaming of milk means success in love affairs.

Mirror—To see yourself in the glass denotes wounded pride or sickness. To break one, misadventure.

Money—To find money means bad luck; to give it away or spend it indicates success.

Monkey—Means "Beware of getting into mischief!"

Moon—To see the full moon denotes fidelity and joy; to see a crescent means awakening affection. An eclipse of the moon means loss.

Mourning—To dream of wearing mourning indicates an invitation to a wedding.

Mud—To find yourself in mud means the coming of wealth.

Mule—Seeing or riding a mule is a sure sign of difficulty.

Murder—To witness a murder means that you will soon see an old friend; to dream of being murdered means caution.

Music—Hearing music in your sleep is a sign of luck.

Mustard—Eating mustard denotes pain and trouble.

N

Nails—Metal nails mean success; finger nails denote misadventures.

Nakedness—Threatened danger and poverty.

Necklace—Receiving one denotes jealousy and annoyance. If a girl wears a necklace she will soon wed.

Needles—Are a sign of disappointment in love.

Nest—Seeing a nest with eggs denotes a quarrel. A nest with birds in it, good luck.

Newspaper—Reading a paper means beware of gossip.

Nose—Dreaming of your own or someone's nose denotes a new acquaintance.

Nurse—Dreaming of a nurse is a sign of long life.

Nuts—Eating nuts denotes a voyage.

O

Oars—Indicate a safe enterprise.

Oaths—A man using blasphemous words signifies trouble.

Offer of Marriage—Denotes happiness for at least a year.

Oil—To dream of oil is a sign of good harvest and prosperity.

Olives—Indicate honors and dignity.

Onions—To dream of eating them means aggravation and disgrace.

Opera—To dream of being at the opera denotes temporary pleasure.

Orange—To eat an orange is a sign of coming amusement.

Orange Blossoms—To see or wear orange blossoms foretells a wedding.

Orchard—To see or be in an orchard signifies a successful business deal.

Ostrich—To dream of an ostrich means failure thru vanity.

Owl—To dream of an owl means that important secrets will be revealed.

Oyster—To dream of opening an oyster denotes honor; eating one foretells a feast.

P

Pail—To carry a pail signifies a new acquaintance. If full it means gain.

Pain—To dream of suffering pain foretells a sickness and a speedy recovery.

Painter—Denotes that your business affairs will improve.

Palm Tree—Denotes honor and victory.

Paper—To dream of reading a newspaper means that happiness will be brief.

Parasol—To carry one denotes a voyage.

Parent—To dream of either father or mother means good news.

Parrot—To dream of a parrot foretells a robbery.

Pastry—To dream of eating pastry denotes annoyance; to bake pastry means improvement in your condition.

Pawnbroker—To go to a pawnbroker signifies a serious loss.

Peaches—To dream of eating peaches denotes pleasure and contentment.

Peacock—Foretells victory.

Peanuts—To eat peanuts signifies a lawsuit.

Pearls—To dream of receiving or wearing pearls signifies tears and distress.

Pears—Eating pears means long life and happiness.

Peas—To dream of peas means good fortune.

Pen—To dream of holding or writing with a pen means good tidings.

Pepper—To dream of pepper denotes affliction.

Pheasant—To kill a pheasant is a sign of good luck.

Piano—Playing on a piano denotes a speedy wedding. Buying one signifies money from an unexpected debt.

Pig—To dream of a pig is a sign of good luck.

Pigsty—Indicates financial gain.

Pigeon—Seeing a pigeon in flight means reconciliation; at rest denotes success.

Pillow—To dream of lying on a pillow indicates sickness.

Pills—Taking pills is a sure sign of trouble and famine.

Pine Tree—Dreaming of a lonely pine tree foretells danger.

Pins—To dream of pins is considered fortunate and means wealth.

Pirate—Foretells a fortunate adventure.

Pistol—To carry a pistol or revolver denotes a change in your prospects for the better.

Pitch—Signifies "Beware of evil companions!"

Pitchfork—Means you will be punished.

Policeman—Is a sure sign of impending trouble.

Postman—Indicates good news, from abroad.

Poverty—To dream that you are poor denotes an unexpected addition to your wealth.

Present—Dreaming of receiving gifts denotes a loss. To make a present means success.

Preserves—To make or eat preserves indicates loss of time and money.

Priest—To dream of a priest denotes reconciliation with an enemy.

Procession—To watch a parade or procession means success in love.

Pump—To pump water is a sign of a speedy marriage.

Purse—An empty purse denotes that you will soon receive a present; a full purse signifies a serious loss.

Q

Quail—To see a quail denotes responsibilities in the family.

Quarrel—Means constancy and friendship.

Queen—To dream of a queen or princess is a sure sign of prosperity.

Quince—To dream of fresh or preserved quinces denotes a scandal.

Quoits—A warning not to gamble.

R

Rabbit—A running rabbit is a sign of disappointment.

Race—To witness a race denotes success in life.

Radish—To pick or eat a radish denotes a secret which you will shortly learn.

Railroad—A token that you will change your residence soon.

Rain—Is a sign of reconciliation with an enemy.

Rainbow—To see a rainbow denotes that better days are coming. It is a very good omen.

Rat—Beware of secret enemies.

Raven—To hear a raven croak portends misfortune.

Reading—To dream of reading a book is a sign that you are too lazy to succeed.

Revenge—Denotes a speedy repentance.

Ribbons—To dream of wearing ribbons is a sign of a visit from one you love.

Rice—To dream of eating or throwing rice denotes, the marriage of an intimate friend.

Ride—To ride with either men or women denotes coming trouble.

Ring—To receive one means a gain; to place one on the finger of another denotes marital trouble.

Rival—To dream of a rival is a sign that you will quarrel with the one you love best.

River—To see a river denotes a change in your condition; to fall into one means "Beware of your enemies!"

Robber—To be attacked by robbers is a sign of victory over a rival.

Rock—Sure sign of annoyance and loss.

Rose—This is always a sign of good luck. White roses signify constancy; red, an offer of marriage.

Rosebush—Denotes a constant lover.

Ruins—To explore a ruin denotes a pleasant surprise.

S

Sailor—To dream of a sailor means good tidings from other lands.

Salad—Means "Beware of embarrassment!"

Salt—To dream of using salt means a rapid recovery of a sick friend; to spill salt denotes disappointment.

Sausage—Is a sign of affliction or sickness.

Saw—Portends a satisfactory end in your affairs.

Scissors—Denotes that a friend will become an enemy.

Sea—To dream of the sea is a sign of a long journey.

Sermon—To hear a long sermon denotes mental trouble.

Servant—Dreaming of a servant means "Beware of being over-confident!"

Sewing—Means someone is plotting against you.

Sheep—Denotes gain in business.

Shell—A sea shell is a sign of success; a cannon shell, a sign of bad luck.

Ship—If at anchor a ship denotes happiness; if sailing, wishes fulfilled.

Shoes—Denote a speedy journey.

Shroud—To dream of a shroud is a very bad omen and often signifies death.

Sickness—To dream of being ill is always a bad sign.

Singing—To sing in your sleep denotes vexation when awake.

Skating—To dream of skating is a sign of success.

Skeleton—The vision of a skeleton usually signifies a change for the better.

Sleep—To dream that you are asleep indicates false security, and is a sign to be cautious.

Slip or Fall—Indicates a rise in position.

Slipper—Is significant of comfort and satisfaction.

Smoke—To smoke a cigar denotes extravagant expectations; to see smoke come out of a chimney denotes gain thru new efforts.

Snail—A crawling snail is a sign of coming dishonor.

Snake—Denotes treason, and is a caution to be careful whom you trust.

Sneezing—Is a sign of long life.

Snow—To see a falling snow signifies a visit from a lovely person.

Soap—Denotes pleasant revelations.

Soldier—To meet a soldier is a sign of a coming quarrel.

Spider—To see a spider spinning its web denotes success in business.

Spirit—To see a spirit in a dream is a caution to be more considerate of those around you.

Sponge—Is a sign of greed and avarice.

Spy—To dream of a spy means "Beware of idle rumors!"

Stable—To dream of a stable denotes a welcome.

Stars—To dream of a star means happiness; a shooting-star, gain of money.

Stocking—To put on or take off a stocking denotes a change in your fortune.

Stones—To dream of throwing stones denotes suffering.

Stork—Seeing a stork means loss thru robbery.

Storm—Being caught in a storm denotes coming vexation.

Stove—Sitting near a stove is an indication of comfort and wealth.

Strange Room—Coming into a strange room denotes the solving of a mystery.

Straw—Is an indication of coming poverty.

Strawberries—Are a sign of unexpected good fortune.

Sugar—Denotes want and suffering.

Sun—To dream of the sun is always lucky and portends a happy future.

Supper—To sit at supper means the news of a birth in the family.

Swan—Means that it will be long before you reach your desires.

Swimming—Is a sign of sure enjoyment.

Sword—To dream of wearing one is a sign of honor; to be wounded with one is a sign of misfortune.

T

Table—To sit at a table denotes abundance.

Tailor—Is a portent of unfaithfulness.

Tea—To drink tea means beware of confusion and trouble.

Tears—To shed tears foretells joy and sympathy.

Teeth—To dream of losing your teeth foretells the death of a friend or the loss of money.

Tent—To dream of being under a tent denotes a quarrel.

Theater—Being at a theater is a sign of coming sadness or loss.

Thimble—Denotes hard work to achieve success.

Thirst—To dream of being thirsty is a sign of affliction.

Thistle—To pluck a thistle foretells a dispute.

Thorn—Is a sign of loss of money.

Thunder—To dream of a thunderstorm denotes danger or death to a friend.

Tiger—To meet a tiger is a warning against an enemy.

Toads—Dreaming of a toad means you will be disgusted with something that will happen to you.

Torch—Denotes an invitation to a wedding.

Treasure—Finding a treasure or a heap of money indicates a disappointment.

Trees—Dreaming of trees denotes "Keep up your courage."

Turkey—To dream of a turkey is a sign of plenty.

Turnips—Denote disappointment and annoyance.

Turtle—To see a turtle is a sign of luck.

Twins—The coming of twins denotes honors and wealth.

U

Umbrella—To borrow one denotes prosperity; to carry one in a storm, you will be beloved.

Uncle—To dream of an uncle denotes an advantageous marriage.

Unfaithful—Dreaming that your sweetheart is unfaithful is a sure sign of true love.

Uniform—To wear a uniform is a sign of coming honors.

Urn—If it contains flowers it means a speedy marriage of someone in your family. Empty, it means a loss.

V

Veil—To wear a white veil means a proposal of marriage; a black veil indicates death or separation.

Vermin—Denotes plenty and prosperity.

Village—Walking thru a village denotes a trip abroad.

Vine—A sign of prosperity and fruitfulness.

Vinegar—To dream of drinking vinegar signifies sickness.

Violet—Denotes fidelity on the part of your sweetheart and success in your undertaking.

Violin—Denotes sympathy and consolation.

Vise—To use a vise indicates wealth through industry.

Visitor—To dream of a visit foreshadows trouble; if others visit you, loneliness.

Voice—To dream of hearing a voice means that absent ones are thinking of you.

Voyage—Is a sign of a coming event that will alter your conditions.

W

Wagon—Denotes ease and pleasure.

Wall—Seeing a wall over which you cannot climb means prosperity after much effort.

War—To dream of war denotes peace and prosperity.

Washing—Washing your clothes denotes that a misunderstanding will soon pass away.

Wasps—Are a sign of annoyance and disappointment.

Watch—To dream of a watch means disappointment, and is a caution to use your time to better advantage.

Watchman—To see a watchman denotes a trifling loss.

Water—To dream of water in any shape is a sign of improvement in your condition.

Waves—To see waves at sea denotes that someone is trying to take advantage of you.

Wedding—To dream that you are at a wedding is often a sign of a funeral; if at your own wedding, it means a change of residence.

Well—To draw water from a well means success in your undertakings.

Wheat—Indicates a gain of much money.

Wheelbarrow—Is a sign of disability or infirmity. If broken it signifies loss.

Wife—If a man dreams that his wife is married to another it is a sign of a quarrel that may be serious.

Window—Looking out of a window is a sign of bad luck.

Wine—To dream of drinking wine means a disappointment; to become intoxicated means disgrace.

Wolf—To see a wolf is a sign of coming poverty. To be attacked by a wolf the defeat of your enemies.

Woman—To dream of a fair woman, beware of deceit; an ugly woman, beware of scandal.

Woods—To walk thru the woods is a sure sign of success.

Work—Dreaming of hard work denotes prosperity.

Worms—Seeing worms is a sign of coming ill health.

Writing—To dream of writing a letter indicates that someone is anxious to hear from you; writing a book, foretells fame.

X

Xmas—To dream of Christmas is a happy omen, and means success in love.

Y

Yacht—To dream of being on a yacht denotes an important letter soon to be received.

Yeast—Is a sign of abundance.

Youth—An old person dreaming of being young means a reunion with an absent friend. A young girl dreaming of a youth can prepare for a speedy marriage.

Z

Zebra—To see one means you will travel abroad; to ride on one, means "Beware of loss!"

Zephyr—To embroider or crochet with zephyr or wool denotes a meeting with a person who will love you.

www.ingramcontent.com/pod-product-compliance
Lightning Source LLC
LaVergne TN
LVHW041500070426
835507LV00009B/715